MW00640264

THE
SOUND
OF
TROUBLE

**Turning the Sound of Trouble
Into the Sound of Triumph!**

Bishop Roger L. Tatuem

The Sound of Trouble
Copyright © 2021
ISBN: 978-0-578-97525-2
Bishop Roger L. Tatuem
Helping Hands Ministries
3237 Level Road
Churchville, MD 21028

FOREWORD

No matter how critically they are examined, Bishop Roger Tatuem's credentials are impeccable. The words *faithful*, *tireless*, and *compassionate* describe his lifetime of service to the body of Christ.

He has been part of the fellowship of churches and ministries under my leadership since its inception, formerly known as World Harvest Ministerial Alliance, now called City Harvest Network. Bishop Tatuem has consistently been one of our most fervent and loyal supporters.

He knows how to serve under the leadership of others, and he also knows how to lead others, having founded and pastored Helping Hands Ministries in Churchville, Maryland.

As impressive as his resume is, what makes him uniquely qualified to write this book is that he has proven these principles in the arena of life's daily conflict. He does not share theoretical or theological principles thought up in an ivory tower far from the battlefield. My friend, Bishop Roger Tatuem, will show you how to turn the sound of trouble into the sound of triumph!

Dr. Rod Parsley, Pastor
World Harvest Church
Columbus, Ohio

INTRODUCTION

It's three o'clock in the morning, and you are awakened from a deep sleep by the jarring sound of the phone ringing. You know it's not an invitation to dinner! *That* sound at *that* time usually means trouble.

You are driving to the grocery store and hear sirens and see flashing lights behind you. You realize you might have been driving too fast, or maybe it is a fire engine or an ambulance. Either way, that sound means trouble.

It's a stormy night—the wind is blowing, the lightning is flashing, and the thunder is rolling. You open the front door and listen for the sound of a tornado warning.

We have been conditioned to respond in certain ways to certain sounds. If the doorbell rings, we answer the door. If the noon whistle blows, we are ready for lunch. If the baby cries, we pick him up.

Trouble usually announces itself with a sound. The first thought you have when you hear the phone ringing in the middle of the night is "Something must be wrong."

The first thought you have when you hear a fire siren behind you is "There must be a fire somewhere."

And you know that if you hear the tornado warning blaring, you had better take cover—trouble is on the way!

But there *is* a way to change our response to trouble. We can condition ourselves to respond differently when trouble comes our way.

First Peter 5:8 says, "*Be sober, be vigilant; because your adversary the devil walks about like a roaring lion, seeking whom he may devour.*" The enemy may be "out to get us," but we have to remember that he is a defeated foe. Jesus already overcame him two thousand years ago, and we can overcome him as well.

When trouble comes, we can condition ourselves to respond in a way that moves us away from the trouble and toward God. We can learn how to overcome the sound of trouble by releasing the sound of victory—God's Word.

In this book, I am going to share with you what I have learned throughout my walk with God that has brought me through an uncommon amount of trouble and into an uncommon amount of blessing. I am going to show you how:

We can turn the sound of trouble into the sound of triumph!

Bishop Roger L. Tatuem
Churchville, MD

Contents

Chapter 1
Troubled Times

We are living in troubled times. Is there anyone who has not had their share of trouble? We may hear the sound of trouble coming against us from all sides. Here is what the Bible tells us about trouble in Job 14:1:

Man who is born of woman is of few days and full of trouble.

What Is Trouble?

No one can escape trouble—it is a part of the world in which we live. Trouble is what keeps us awake at night. Trouble is what torments our minds with fear. Trouble is everything that comes against us and tries to steal our peace.

The word *trouble* has many meanings:

- *To be troubled* means we are upset, vexed, or worried about something; we are mentally agitated.

1

The Sound of Trouble

- *To trouble* someone is to distress, annoy, or inconvenience them in some way.
- A *trouble* can be a problem, a sickness, or an adverse circumstance.

In spiritual terms, we would call trouble "*a bad report.*" The prophet Isaiah asked a question that we must still answer today: "*Whose report will we believe?*"
Will we believe:

...the evil report that there are giants inhabiting our Promised Land?
...the unrest all around us or the "peace that passes understanding"?
...the test results our doctor sent us or the scripture that tells us "by His stripes, we are healed"?

We can't let trouble get to our hearts. It might mess with our minds, but we can't let it get to our hearts. We bear the responsibility of safeguarding our hearts from the sound of trouble. Jesus told us we would have trouble in this world, but not to be afraid of it. How can we live above the fear?
Here is how: Although we have been *born into a natural world* filled with trouble, we have been *born again into a spiritual kingdom* filled

with overcoming power!

Trouble does not have to destroy people's lives—God has put us here to be an ANSWER in this earth for troubled times. Jesus initiated that process when He told His disciples how to protect their hearts and deal with trouble.

Jesus told them in John 14:1:

Let not your heart be troubled; you believe in God, believe also in Me.

Jesus knew we would face trouble; He knew what it was like to live in this world. He told His disciples not to worry. The same is true for us today. He did not leave us without an answer. Because He overcame trouble, we can, too!

John 16:33 says:

These things I have spoken to you, that in Me you may have peace. In the world you will have tribulation; but be of good cheer, I have overcome the world.

The solution to the problem of trouble is found in the Word of God. It is very important for us as believers to have a filter between what we hear and what we believe.

That filter is the Word of God. We don't have to fear the enemy—if we deal with the fear, we can defeat the enemy. The way we deal with fear is by filtering it through the Word of God.

Fear attracts the things of the devil's kingdom, but faith attracts the things of God's kingdom. The enemy will not be able to bounce us around like ping pong balls if we filter everything through God's Word.

Psalm 27:5 tells us that filtering what we see and hear through the truth of God's Word will have this effect:

For in the time of trouble He shall hide me in His pavilion; In the secret place of His tabernacle He shall hide me; He shall set me high upon a rock.

In our times of mental agitation, when we are vexed and it seems like we cannot think clearly, we can begin to focus in on God's Word, which assures us that He will hide us from our enemy in times of trouble.

Where is that hiding place? What is His pavilion? It is the place of God's presence; it's in His Word.

When our hearts and minds are focused on the Word, Isaiah 26:3 says:

You will keep him in perfect peace, Whose mind is stayed on You.

We can be free from mental agitation; we can be free from vexation. In the time of trouble, we can look to the Word of God. And when others see that we are free, we can point them to this same source of freedom.

How will they know we are free? Freedom announces itself. People will seldom follow a weak voice, but they will take heed to a voice filled with power and confidence.

Consider what 1 Corinthians 14:8 says:

For if the trumpet makes an uncertain sound, who will prepare for battle?

What is Sound?

When people hear us confidently speaking the Word of God, it will be a sound they can recognize and identify. A rallying cry is never soft and timid, but strong and confident. Speaking the Word of God gives a clear and certain sound. Sound, like trouble, has several meanings:

- A *sound* is something we can hear.
- Something that is *sound* is secure and reliable—a *sound* decision.
- To be *sound* is to be well and whole.

The Sound of Trouble

Speaking the Word of God encompasses all these meanings. Hearing the physical sounds of the Word being spoken will produce a spiritual soundness—an impression of wellness, security, and wholeness.

Sound enters our ear gate and is analyzed, or interpreted, by our minds. That interpretation depends on the filter through which our minds operate, our perception and understanding of what a word, or phrase or sentence means, and how it makes us feel.

The sounds we hear could signify trouble, or they could signify blessing. That is why it is so important that the sounds we release are not the sounds of trouble and defeat but sounds of victory and faith. Sounds of trouble lead to fear, but sounds of faith lead to victory. Our assignment is to lead people *out of* fear, and *into* faith!

We have the answer for those who are in trouble. The first step in dealing with trouble is to believe in God. Jesus said that if we believe in God, we should also believe in Him (John 14:1). Our Heavenly Father does not want His people to have trouble. Throughout the Bible, we see God delivering His people *out of* trouble, even after they had gotten themselves into it.

The reality is that there will always be trouble in the world, but as believers, we don't always have to be in a world of trouble! Jesus came into the world to take care of trouble—all kinds of trouble, not the least of which was the sin problem that separated God and man. In doing so, He told us not to be afraid of the sound of trouble, but to have faith in the Word of God, and in what He had accomplished on the cross.

We don't have to be overcome by the fear of trouble, but we can overcome fear with our faith. Jesus overcame; we can overcome. We don't have to let our hearts be troubled, we believe in God, and we believe also in Christ Jesus. We don't have to live our lives in *fear*; we can live our lives in *faith*.

We can turn the sound of trouble into the sound of triumph!

Chapter 2
Secret Plots of the Wicked

There is an antidote for the sound of trouble: the Word of God. The enemy does not want you to know this. He wants to keep his methods secret and keep you from discovering this lifesaving truth.

Psalm 64:1 says:

Hear my voice, O God, in my meditation;
Preserve my life from fear of the enemy.

The Psalm writer did not ask God to preserve his life *from* the enemy, he asked God to preserve him from the *fear* of the enemy. Fear is devastating, and fear has torment.

What is the fear of the enemy? What generates that fear? The source of the fear is what the enemy *says* that he is going to do to us. It's the threat of the torment and devastation he says he is going to bring upon us. It is the sound of the words he plants in our minds that play over and over again—it's the sound of trouble.

That sound will automatically open the door

to fear if we allow it. If we listen to his sound and analyze what it means without a filter—without running it through the filter of the Word of God—we will interpret it as trouble. Once we decide that the sound means trouble, we can be easily persuaded to open the door to fear.

It's more than just the sound that we're hearing; it's the feelings of torment, uneasiness, or nervousness that accompany it. Fear is a spirit, and before the enemy ever gets to us, the spirit of fear will confront us.

Fear can defeat us before the actual trouble ever shows up. We've all seen the old movies where one of the characters, when given bad news, clutches their chest and falls to the floor dead. Although it seems overly melodramatic on the screen, such things can and do happen in real life. A person's system can become flooded with adrenaline in a desperate moment, and their heart can stop.

But this doesn't have to happen to us. Faith replaces fear when we filter what we hear through the Word of God. Most of the time, the things the enemy taunts us with aren't even real, they are only **F**alse **E**vidence **A**ppearing **R**eal.

Everything that is seen in creation began in the spirit world before it ever manifested in the natural world. Trouble is the same. Trouble begins in the spiritual realm. It is a spiritual force long before it manifests in the natural.

Here is the answer: when the sound of trouble comes, we filter it through the Word of God. We can take those worries and anxieties that the enemy presents to us and look to God's Word for an answer. We can be like David, and say, *"Preserve my life from fear of the enemy."*

Let's continue to look at Psalm 64. Read on to verse 2:

Hide me from the secret plots of the wicked, From the rebellion of the workers of iniquity.

The Workers of Iniquity

Who are these workers of iniquity? According to the Word of God, these wicked ones are agents of the enemy who are secretly plotting against us. They don't want us to know what they are doing, or how to defeat them. They don't want us to find out that we can speak the Word of God against them and destroy their evil works. They don't want us to believe God's Word and speak it against them.

Psalm 64:3 compares the tongue to a deadly weapon:

Who sharpen their tongue like a sword, And bend their bows to shoot their arrows— bitter words.

The Sound of Trouble

When we own a weapon, we learn how to take care of it, and we learn how to use it. We practice with it. We clean it. We shine it up, and we get it ready. We make sure it will not misfire on us.

The workers of iniquity are not just sitting back and watching, they are practicing their craft and perfecting their technique. Look at the words that follow the word *arrows*. "*Bitter words.*" This tells us what the arrows really are.

James 3:8 says:

But no man can tame the tongue. It is an unruly evil, full of deadly poison.

Mankind can tame the beasts of the field, the birds of the air, and the creatures of the sea, but he cannot tame the tongue. The only way the tongue can be tamed is by using it to speak the Word of God.

The workers of iniquity are not attacking the guilty; they are attacking the innocent. Don't think that the enemy will leave us alone because we are "good Christians."

Let's read on in Psalm 64:4:

That they may shoot in secret at the blameless; Suddenly they shoot at him and do not fear.

We are the ones the enemy targets. He wants to silence us before we can bring hurt or damage to his kingdom. He doesn't want us to become effective at using the Word of God against him. He has his weapon of fear, and he is not afraid to use it. Why should he be afraid of us if we have been silenced and don't know how to use our weapons? He will continue to shoot at us without fear.

We would expect him to use the unsaved to come against us. We would not expect him to use the saved ones around us. In Psalm 55:14, King David laments the pain of this kind of betrayal from someone with whom he "*took sweet counsel together*" and with whom he "*walked unto the house of God in company.*"

David said that it wasn't the wicked or the enemy that got next to him. It was his brother— the one who went into the sanctuary with him, the one who had worshipped right beside him— the one who had been recruited by the enemy.

Psalm 64:5 reminds us that misery loves company:

They encourage themselves in an evil matter; They talk of laying snares secretly; They say, "Who will see them?"

These evil workers will always look for someone to agree with them, someone they can use to help them accomplish their evil plans. They don't want to see us do well. They don't want to see us make progress. They don't want to see us grow in God. They will give themselves a pep talk to help them carry out their evil deeds.

They sharpen their tongues to shoot out bitter words, trying to discourage us and wound us. Sharp arrows (remember, these are *words*) *can* wound us. They don't just inflict surface damage; their wounds run deep. Bitter words can strike us at the core of our life and demobilize us. They can make us want to give up on God and withdraw from everybody in the world.

That is why we have to be mindful and deliberate about what we say to people. We can't afford to let the enemy use us to speak words that will wound a brother or sister in Christ. Our words should be used to cover and protect each other, and to pray and intercede for each other.

The workers of iniquity want to shoot in secret. They don't have the guts to come out in the open. They are the ones whispering behind the scenes, attempting to exert their influence overtly.

Then, they will try to draw God into their mess. They will try to get us to blame God for what is going on in our lives. They want to shift the blame for their evil works on to God when He didn't have anything to do with it.

Although we know the Bible says that the light will expose the evil deeds that are done in darkness, we still have to walk circumspectly and be on guard against the plans of the enemy.

We can't allow the sound of trouble to produce fear in us. We can change that sound by speaking the Word of God and saying: "God has not given me the spirit of fear" (2 Timothy 1:7). We can use the sound of the Word of God to defeat the sound of trouble.

We have to learn how to identify what's going on and learn how to deal with it. We can't allow it to cause us to join the ranks of the wicked just because they shot an arrow into us. There is someplace we can go when the arrows are flying, and it's not into the arms of the enemy. It's not into a place of fretting; it's into the place of faith.

We often tell someone who is undergoing trouble to get up, wash their face, comb their hair, and get dressed. When they do this, it will begin to lift their spirits right away.

We can do the same thing in the spirit realm—we can get dressed! God gave us an outfit for times like this—the helmet of salvation, the breastplate of righteousness, the loin belt of truth, the shield of faith, and the sword of the spirit.

This is not the time for *moping*; it is the time for *hoping*. It is the time to remind ourselves to hope in God. We are to speak *hope* to ourselves. Psalm 42:5 says:

Why are you cast down, O my soul? And why are you disquieted within me? Hope in God, for I shall yet praise Him For the help of His countenance.

This admonition is so important that it is repeated in Psalm 43:5:

Why are you cast down, O my soul? And why are you disquieted within me? Hope in God; For I shall yet praise Him, The help of my countenance and my God.

As we begin processing the onslaught of the enemy through the filter of the Word of God, hope will arise in our hearts. Now, it's time to put on the garment of praise and begin to praise the One who is our hope and our help.

The Sound of Praise

The enemy will try to instill fear. He will try to intimidate us with the sound of trouble. But when we know who we are and who lives on the inside of us, we know that we are kept by God's divine power. When trouble comes, we can speak the Word of God in faith.

Jehoshaphat, King of Judah, had an experience like this. There were several tribes that God would not let the children of Israel invade and conquer as they possessed the Promised Land. Now these very same tribes— the ones who had been spared—were preparing to attack them.

Second Chronicles 20:3 tells us:

And Jehoshaphat feared, and set himself to seek the LORD, and proclaimed a fast throughout all Judah.

After the people had assembled together and fasted and prayed, Jahaziel the prophet gave them a word from the Lord (2 Chronicles 20:17):

You will not need to fight in this battle. Position yourselves, stand still and see the salvation of the LORD, who is with you, O Judah and Jerusalem! Do not fear or be dismayed; tomorrow go out against them, for the LORD is with you.

The people of God need to come together when bad reports come in. We shouldn't go running off to the arms of flesh—we just need to get together with other believers who know how to operate in the Kingdom of God.

17

The Sound of Trouble

That is what Jehoshaphat did as his forces prepared to go up against their enemies—he called for the best singers and praisers and put them out in front of the army. This was the vanguard of the army of Judah!

It came to pass exactly as the prophet had declared. They went forth singing the praises of God, standing still and watching as their enemies slaughtered each other, and God gave them the victory.

The name *Judah* means *praise*. Judah was the fourth son of Jacob and Leah, and his name meant "I will praise." His mother gave him that name because her heart was full of praise for all the sons that God had given her. His name also became the name of the southern kingdom of Israel when the land was divided into two kingdoms.

So, when we encounter trouble, we can call on Judah. Praise is one of the elements that will help us deal with the sound of trouble. When we put Judah to work on the sound of trouble, we don't have to fight the battle, because the battle is the Lord's. We hold our peace, and the Lord will fight our battles.

We don't sing songs of unbelief; we sing songs that say what God's Word says. God will defeat His enemies through the sound of singing and the sound of musical instruments.

Here is one result that we can expect, recorded in Isaiah 30:29-32, when we come before the Lord with singing and praise:

You shall have a song As in the night when a holy festival is kept, And gladness of heart as when one goes with a flute, To come into the mountain of the LORD, To the Mighty One of Israel. The Lord will cause His glorious voice to be heard . . . For through the voice of the LORD, Assyria will be beaten down, As He strikes with the rod.

When the instruments are playing and the praise team is singing, the Bible says that the Lord is sending a crushing blow down on the heads of the Assyrians, who here represent an enemy kingdom.

When the enemy sends a sound of trouble, we can go against him with the sound of praise. We won't let the sound of trouble stop us. We won't let him tell us we are defeated before we ever see the smoking gun. The enemy's secret plots are uncovered and rendered powerless against us when we speak the Word of God and give God praise. We can praise our way through anything, and God will give us the victory!

We can turn the sound of trouble into the sound of triumph!

Chapter 3
The Lion's Roar

The giant came down from the top of the mountain, confronting the armies of Israel who were hiding in the trenches and cowering in fear. He was over nine feet tall, wearing armor that must have weighed nearly as much as a man. His voice was as loud as the roar of a lion, and it reverberated throughout the valley.

The words he was shouting at the Israelites were terrifying: "Send me a man who will fight me! Send out a man who can defeat me, and you can go free—our armies won't have to fight each other. But if he fails, you will be defeated, and you will have to serve us."

This was undoubtedly the sound of trouble! The Philistines had gathered their armies together to come against Israel. The giant, Goliath, was their most imposing warrior. His mere presence was enough to strike fear in the hearts of the soldiers. King Saul and all the Israelites were terrified of this giant of a man.

To them, his threats were as terrifying as the roar of a lion.

Like a Roaring Lion

One of the most distinguishing traits of a lion is its ability to roar. Think about the sound of a roar: it is loud, it is deep, it is wild. Few animals can roar; the roar of the lion is the loudest of all. The sound of that roar can travel many miles.

The loud, deep roar of a lion is the sound of trouble in the wild. The lion's roar is known and recognized throughout its habitat. A lion is always seeking its next meal—when the roar of the lion is heard, its prey scatters.

In the same way, the enemy of our souls is always seeking his next victim. The Bible teaches us to watch and pray so that when trouble comes, we can hear the sound and identify the source.

First Peter 5:8 says:

Be sober, be vigilant; because your adversary the devil walks about like a roaring lion, seeking whom he may devour.

Once we identify the source, we can change the outcome. If we can identify him through his sound, we can defeat him.

Second Corinthians 2:11 says:

Lest Satan should take advantage of us; for we are not ignorant of his devices.

Like a lion who preys on weak, small, or isolated animals, the enemy uses a similar tactic. He knows when the door has been left open, and he will use that knowledge to take advantage of us—if we let him. If we don't close that door, the devil will accomplish his tri-fold effort to steal, kill, and destroy. That is why we have to be diligent to give no place to the devil (Ephesians 4:27).

John 10:10 says:

The thief does not come except to steal, and to kill, and to destroy. I have come that they may have life, and that they may have it more abundantly.

If we want to walk in that abundant life, we need to keep the enemy out. Are we speaking negatively? Start speaking the Word instead—and close the door. Have we offended someone? Ask their forgiveness—and close the door. Have we lied or gotten involved in gossip? Speak the truth in love—and close the door.

God has given us a strong and powerful weapon to use against the tactics of the devil. We can exercise our authority over him by speaking the Word of God. But if he can make us afraid, he can stop us from using the Word of God against him. God has given us a weapon, but it's up to us to use it.

The lion will study the habits of its prey and stalk them until it finds them in a vulnerable position, then it goes in for the kill. The enemy operates in the same manner—he sends out his familiar spirits to learn our weaknesses. He has made it his business to know our family history. He studies our family's characteristics and our family's mannerisms. He knows how to pass those characteristics on from generation to generation. In any family tree, we can recognize patterns and cycles where problems, issues, and addictions have been passed from one generation to the next.

It is said that the roar of a lion will paralyze its prey. When the devil sends his trouble, it comes with a roar. The roar is meant to instill fear in us. It is meant to cause us to let down our guard and allow the enemy free reign to destroy us. The Bible tells us that these times will come to test our faith.

First Peter 4:12 says:

Beloved, do not think it strange concerning the fiery trial which is to try you, as though some strange thing happened to you.

We can take our stand on the Word of God. We were not made to be defeated by the devil. We were not made to be influenced or affected through others by the devil. The first thing the enemy does is roar. He wants to stop us in our tracks.

Isaiah 5:29 says:

Their roaring will be like a lion, They will roar like young lions; Yes, they will roar And lay hold of the prey; They will carry it away safely, And no one will deliver.

Just as the lion studies its prey, the enemy will study us. He will put together a strategy to ambush and devour us. When the enemy brings us bad news, we can come against him with the good news of God's Word.

Ephesians 6:16 says:

Above all, taking the shield of faith with which you will be able to quench all the fiery darts of the wicked one.

When the enemy throws his fiery darts, they will hit the shield of faith—the Word that we have spoken—and die out.

Lion Fighters

We were not made to walk in defeat; we were made to walk in victory—no matter what the circumstances may look like.

David was a young man who understood this principle. He had already experienced the power of God in his life, having killed both a lion and a bear. Even though all the armies of Saul were trembling with fear in the presence of Goliath, David knew his God was more powerful than a mere giant!

Just like David, we were created to be conquerors—lion and bear slayers, and giant killers. We are part of the root of Jesse, from the household of David (Isaiah 11:10).

When David heard Goliath taunting the armies of Israel, he recognized the sound of trouble. He knew from his past experience that his God would be with him during times of trouble. He learned early in life the lessons he would need as he moved into his future calling as King of Israel.

But, in this moment, what he knew, and what he was certain of, was that God would be with him if he took action against the uncircumcised Philistine who stood in front of him. David was not going to allow the words of one man—even a giant of a man—to defy his God and destroy the armies of Israel.

David was well-acquainted with his God. If we will acquaint ourselves with God, and with His Word, there is nothing the enemy can do to us.

The mental impression left by the thoughts and words that the enemy tries to place in our hearts can destroy our motivation to fight for what we believe. The enemy's ways, left unchecked, will always lead to death—the death of a dream, the death of hope, even the death of the body.

However, Proverbs 18:21 tells us:

Death and life are in the power of the tongue.

David understood this principle. He saw and heard the same sights and sounds of trouble that his brothers saw and heard. He saw and heard the same sights and sounds of trouble that the armies of Israel saw and heard.

- *He saw the size of Goliath.*
- *He heard the giant's threats.*
- *He perceived the fear that it instilled in the armies of Israel.*

He saw and heard the effect of the sound of trouble coming from the mouth of the giant.

None of that *moved* him more than his faith in God *motivated* him.

Like David, we can take up the same challenge and conquer the sound of trouble. Even though everyone around him told him he was not equal to the task, his faith in God told him that he was.

We need to be clear in our thinking and know that the devil can, indeed, be a lethal enemy. But also need to be clear in our understanding that he is a defeated foe. We can study the Word of God to know him and his devices so that we can maintain the victory given to us when Jesus defeated him on the cross of Calvary.

With faith in our hearts, and the Word of God in our mouths, we can, like David, slay lions, bears, and even the giants that the devil places before us.

> *We can turn the sound of trouble*
> *into the sound of triumph!*

Chapter 4
The Fiery Trial

The Bible tells us in 1 Peter 4:12 not to think the trials that come upon us are strange. We are not exempt from trials; they have been happening throughout history—they only appear to be strange:

Beloved, do not think it strange concerning the fiery trial which is to try you, as though some strange thing happened to you.

The Kingdom of God has been under assault from the very beginning. It began when Lucifer wanted to take over heaven. The words he spoke revealed the wickedness in his heart.

Listen to what he said, recorded in Isaiah 14:13-14:

For you have said in your heart: 'I will ascend into heaven, I will exalt my throne above the stars of God; I will also sit on the mount of the congregation On the farthest sides of the north; I will ascend above the heights of the clouds, I will be like the Most High.'

Lucifer's expressed desire was to be like God, and to rule in heaven. His words were so convincing that one-third of the angels followed after him. He spoke the sound of trouble, but God cancelled that plan by speaking His word against it. Here, recorded in the next verse, is what God said to Lucifer:

Yet you shall be brought down to Sheol, To the lowest depths of the Pit.

Revelation 12:9 records the fulfillment of God's words:

So the great dragon was cast out, that serpent of old, called the Devil and Satan, who deceives the whole world; he was cast to the earth, and his angels were cast out with him.

God Himself faced an attack and overcame an adversary with His words. He has shown us by example in His Word how to deal with fiery trials. He spoke, and His words canceled the plans of the devil, providing us with a model and an example we can follow. God has informed us that trials will come, and He has prepared us so that we can be ready when they do.

Afflictions and Deliverance

Psalm 34:19 begins with what we might look at as unwelcome news:

Many are the afflictions of the righteous...

Thankfully, the verse does not end there. The Psalmist David continues:

...But the Lord delivers him out of them all.

The devil will test us by speaking negative words to us. He wants us to believe him, not our Heavenly Father. But we can be assured by this verse that no matter what kind of trials come, God has given us a way to deal with the enemy's attack.

The enemy will announce the circumstances he plans to bring against us, then he will tell us the negative impact they are going to have on us. These words are only the *sound* of trouble. It is at this point that we can begin to counter the sound of trouble with the sound of the Word of God.

The enemy cannot tell the truth because the truth is not in him. The Bible calls him the father of lies (John 8:44). Jesus, however, calls Himself "*the way, the truth, and the life*" (John 14:6). To know the truth—and to speak the truth that we know—will cancel the devastation that was intended by the sound of trouble.

The more of the Word of God that we hide in our heart before the trials come, the more truth we will know, and the more effective we will be at speaking that truth. Fiery trials are going to come, but that's not the end of the story.

First Peter 4:13 says:

> *But rejoice to the extent that you partake of Christ's sufferings, that when His glory is revealed, you may also be glad with exceeding joy.*

This verse gives us additional instruction on how to counter the sound of trouble. This verse tells us to rejoice when we encounter the trials, and the glory of what Christ has done for us will be revealed.

As it says in 1 Peter 4:1, we rejoice because the trial will reveal a marvelous truth: Christ has already suffered for us and has given us the victory:

> *Therefore, since Christ suffered for us in the flesh, arm yourselves also with the same mind.*

We can operate according to God's will for us. We can adopt a heavenly mindset and arm ourselves with the mind of Christ. We don't have to yield to the sound of trouble, we can counteract it by rejoicing and speaking the Word.

Be Strong In The Lord

But we can't give up. We need to stay "*strong in the Lord, and in the power of His might*" (Ephesians 6:10). No matter how loud the sound of trouble is, or how much trouble shows up, we have an antidote. We can beat the trouble.

In times of trouble, the Bible says that God will hide us, and He will lift us up above our enemies. What an amazing promise. Jesus' victory becomes our victory, and all that is left is the rejoicing!

Let's look at a well-known Bible story and see this principle in action. We are familiar with the story of the three Hebrew boys who were thrown into the fiery furnace. These three boys—Shadrach, Meshach, and Abednego— were taken, along with others, from their own country and held in bondage by Nebuchadnezzar, the King of Babylon. They were highly intelligent young men, and they were soon promoted to watch over the affairs of the king.

The problem occurred when they refused to bow down to the image of the king and worship him. The penalty for this was being thrown into a fiery furnace. This would qualify by anyone's reckoning as a "*fiery trial*," and a *strange* one, at that.

Shadrach, Meshach, and Abednego told the king that their God would deliver them. They were counteracting the sound of trouble with the sound of faith.

The three Hebrews boys believed their God would save them. Believers *should* believe—this is the only way God can work on our behalf and bring the possible out of the impossible.

Mark 9:23 says:

If you can believe, all things are possible to him who believes.

We can always believe God, no matter how severe the sound of trouble might be. He will bring us *out of the trouble* if we will bring Him *into the trouble* by speaking His Word.

They did not bow, nor did they burn. They honored the God of Israel, whom they served. They knew Him, they knew His promises for their nation, and they spoke accordingly. He supernaturally delivered them from the fiery furnace into which they had been thrown. This was a strange trial, and a fiery one, but they still came out victorious.

Several amazing things happened when God delivered them: the fire could not burn them, and the smell of the smoke could not stay on them, and all could see a fourth man in the fire, walking with them. Their God had come to deliver them!

Daniel 3:27 says:

They saw these men on whose bodies the fire had no power; the hair of their head was not singed nor were their garments affected, and the smell of fire was not on them.

Because of this demonstration of God's power, King Nebuchadnezzar began to bless the Hebrew God, and declare that there was no other God who could deliver like the God of Shadrach, Meshach, and Abednego.

When we face the sound of trouble that comes our way, and begin to speak the Word of God, we, too, will be delivered. Then, as the world around us sees that deliverance, they will have to acknowledge that there is no God like our God!

We can turn the sound of trouble into the sound of triumph!

Chapter 5
Examples of the
Sound of Trouble

We can learn some valuable life lessons by looking at examples of people in the Bible. We can examine how they dealt with the sound of trouble, and whether or not their actions brought them success or failure.

The Defeat of Samson

Samson was an Israelite leader who lived during the 11th century BC. He was a judge in Israel for twenty years. He was known for the exceptional strength that God had given to him.

The Spirit of the Lord would come on Samson and anoint him to do things beyond natural human ability. He killed a young lion with his bare hands. He also slew a thousand Philistine soldiers with the jawbone of a donkey.

Samson was highly anointed by God, but extremely weak in his relationships with women. He was a victim of the sound of trouble.

At this time, his wife was a woman from Timnah. Samson had posed a riddle to a group of thirty young men from her city, promising a reward if they could solve it: he would give them *"thirty linen garments and thirty changes of clothing* (Judges 14:12).

These young men could not answer the riddle, so they threatened to burn Samson's wife and her whole family to death if she did not persuade him to give her the answer to the riddle. After much weeping and crying on her part (the sound of trouble), he finally revealed the answer to her.

She, in turn, revealed it to the young men. Now, Samson had to make good on his word to them. He did this by attacking thirty men of Ashkelon and taking their clothing to give to the thirty young men of Timnah. His actions set off the beginnings of war between Israel and the Philistines.

The sound of trouble often comes in the form of a threat (Judges 14:15). The enemy will use whatever he can to intimidate us and cause us to yield to his devices. However, if we will speak the Word instead—and don't yield—we can have victory over the sound of trouble.

Samson had another run-in with the sound of trouble. The enemy found another woman he could use to bring the sound of trouble to

Samson.

Samson had fallen in love with another beautiful woman named Delilah. Several Philistine men approached Delilah and promised her a great deal of money if she could find out the secret of his strength.

She began to question Samson (the sound of trouble) about his strength. He gave her several different answers, none of which were true.

Eventually, she persuaded him to divulge the truth: were his hair cut off, his strength would be gone as well. Delilah relayed this to the Philistines, and Samson was captured and enslaved. He did have one great rally of strength after his hair grew back, but it came at the cost of his own life.

His gift was gone, and his life was cut short. That is one of the enemy's tactics—to destroy the gift of God within you, and to rob the body of Christ of the benefit of that gift.

Although the stories of Samson's riddle and the secret of his strength didn't end well, the story of Hezekiah's sickness had the opposite result.

Hezekiah's Sound of Trouble

When Hezekiah was king in Israel, God sent him a message through the prophet Isaiah.

Isaiah 38:1 says:

The Sound of Trouble

In those days Hezekiah was sick and near death. And Isaiah the prophet, the son of Amoz, went to him and said to him, "Thus says the LORD: 'Set your house in order, for you shall die and not live.'"

There is no more definite word from God than one announcing a death sentence. If God says we are going to die, then that's it—at least as far as our human understanding goes. For most of us, that proclamation would definitely be the sound of trouble.

However, Hezekiah understood that sincere and effectual prayer was the way to turn the death sentence (the sound of trouble) around. He knew how to touch the heart of God.

Isaiah 38:2-3 says:

Then Hezekiah turned his face toward the wall, and prayed to the LORD, and said, "Remember now, O LORD, I pray, how I have walked before You in truth and with a loyal heart, and have done what is good in Your sight." And Hezekiah wept bitterly.

God heard Hezekiah's prayer and sent Isaiah back to tell him that his prayer had been effective, and that God was adding fifteen years to his life. Hezekiah's prayer against the sound of trouble not only helped him, but it brought about the defeat of an enemy country that was preparing to attack them.

Isaiah 38:4-6 says:

> *And the word of the LORD came to Isaiah, saying, "Go and tell Hezekiah, 'Thus says the LORD, the God of David your father: "I have heard your prayer, I have seen your tears; surely I will add to your days fifteen years. I will deliver you and this city from the hand of the king of Assyria, and I will defend this city."*

Elijah Running from Trouble

Elijah was called as a prophet to both Judah and Israel. His job was to confront the evil rulers of the day who had fallen away from God.

During a showdown on Mount Carmel with the wicked King Ahab, Elijah called fire down from heaven and decreed that all the false prophets of Baal were to be killed.

When Jezebel, the wife of King Ahab, found out what had happened, she threatened to kill Elijah. The sound of this trouble sent him running—away from God, and not toward Him!

First Kings 19:1-5 tells the story:

> *And Ahab told Jezebel all that Elijah had done, also how he had executed all the*

prophets with the sword. Then Jezebel sent a messenger to Elijah, saying, "So let the gods do to me, and more also, if I do not make your life as the life of one of them by tomorrow about this time."

And when he saw that, he arose and ran for his life, and went ... a day's journey into the wilderness, and came and sat down under a broom tree.

And he prayed that he might die, and said, "It is enough! Now, LORD, take my life, for I am no better than my fathers!"

Then as he lay and slept under a broom tree, suddenly an angel touched him, and said to him, "Arise and eat."

That's what the sound of trouble will do. Elijah had allowed so much fear to rule his heart that God had to send an angel to speak to him.

When the enemy comes in, we can be overcome, or we can become an overcomer. We have to put the Word of God back on the trouble.

Eventually, God reassured him that He was still with him—he was not alone. Elijah went on to find and appoint his successor, Elisha, and fulfill all that God had asked him to do.

My Personal Bout with Trouble

The sound of trouble is not exclusive to the men and women in the Bible. I've had my share of negative reports over the years. The sound of trouble came into my life in a dramatic way.

A cardiologist told me in 1983 that I had a deteriorating aortic valve. During the next eleven years, I had regular medical checkups for this condition. I also used God's Word as my medicine. I confessed scriptures that promised healing for my heart.

The Bible says in Psalm 107:20:

He sent His word, and healed them, And delivered them from their destructions.

The condition began to grow worse, and the cardiologist finally told me in 1994 that I had to have open-heart surgery, or I would not live. This was the sound of trouble to me because I was believing God for a supernatural healing. I was afraid to undergo surgery.

Around this time, I went to a live concert in Washington, D.C. God began to minister to me during one of the songs. The words the Holy Spirit spoke to my heart were "*Fear not, little child, for I will take care you.*" I began to cry uncontrollably, and my fears of dying instantly dissipated. I was confident that God would take good care of me through the surgery.

The operation was a major success and the results lasted for 22 years, double the time from my first diagnosis to my first surgery.

However, once again, the sound of trouble came to instill fear in me. A heart catheterization was done and the surgeon who performed the procedure stated that my heart had deteriorated to the point that I would not survive the operation I now needed.

Leading up to the surgery, my wife Miriam and I attended two healing services. God ministered to me supernaturally in both services. This gave me a great deal of peace.

Miriam and I had prayer with the operating surgeon. He announced that he would do the surgery, and with his thirty years of experience and our faith in God, it would be a success.

This surgery was scheduled for fifteen hours, but was completed in four, with a great outcome. Although the sound of trouble came to steal my peace and my life, the sound of prayer and faith cancelled the enemy's plan.

We are not immune to the sound of trouble in this life. However, it is God's plan to deliver us from that trouble.

We can turn the sound of trouble
into the sound of triumph!

Chapter 6
The Sound for Trouble

The antidote for the sound *OF* trouble is the sound *FOR* trouble. God doesn't identify the enemy without giving us the solution.

The sound of trouble creates a mental impression. Initially, it is only in our minds; it has not manifested yet. The words the enemy speaks to us create a mental impression.

Proverbs 23:7 says:

For as he thinks in his heart, so is he.

Renew and Rejoice

What we dwell on is what we will become. That is why we need to "*be renewed*" in our minds (Ephesians 4:23). Our victory begins in our minds. This is not a word to be taken casually; it is a powerful antidote against trouble.

When we renew our minds with the Word of God—and begin to speak that Word—that Word will cover us. The enemy can no longer see us; he sees the One who defeated him, the One who triumphed over him. All he sees is that Word.

Our circumstances are determined by whose words we are listening to and whose words we are speaking.

Proverbs 18:21 says:

Death and life are in the power of the tongue, And those who love it will eat its fruit.

One way to overcome the sound of trouble is to replace it with the sound of joy. We have to substitute what we are hearing that sounds like trouble with something that brings joy and rejoicing—and there is nothing that brings greater joy than the Word of God. We can rejoice that our deliverance is in the Word!

We say what the Word says about us. The gospel is good news—we simply have to learn how to substitute the bad news from the enemy with the good news of the gospel.

Paul says in Romans 1:16:

For I am not ashamed of the gospel of Christ, for it is the power of God to salvation for everyone who believes, for the Jew first and also for the Greek.

The gospel is good news, and this good news is the power of God unto salvation. Salvation refers to the deliverance, security, and safety that God has brought us into: He has delivered us from darkness and brought us into the kingdom of His Son (Colossians 1:13).

When we begin to speak the Word of God, the enemy will try to convince us that it is not working, and that his words are more powerful than God's words. We know that this is not true.

Here are some examples of the higher order of medicine found in God's Word:

Proverbs 4:20-22: *My son, give attention to my words; Incline your ear to my sayings. Do not let them depart from your eyes; Keep them in the midst of your heart; For they are life to those who find them, and health to all their flesh.*

Proverbs 17:22: *A merry heart does good, like medicine, But a broken spirit dries the bones.*

Exodus 15:26: *"... if you diligently heed the voice of the LORD your God and do what is right in His sight ... I will put none of the diseases on you which I have brought on the Egyptians. For I am the LORD who heals you."*

The Sound of Trouble

When the sound of trouble comes to us, or when the enemy tries to attack us by bringing back old symptoms, we can begin to speak the Word of God, and joy will come.

Jeremiah 15:16 says:

Your words were found, and I ate them, And Your word was to me the joy and rejoicing of my heart; For I am called by Your name, O LORD God of hosts.

We will begin to exemplify joy. We will give God the praise because we have taken the antidote. The enemy will try to defeat us by stealing our joy, but he cannot succeed if we will diligently speak the Word and rejoice in God!

Daniel Stayed True

When Jerusalem was besieged by the Babylonians, they took vessels from the house of God, and took in custody certain of the finest young men in the kingdom. One of these young men was Daniel. Daniel 6:3 reads:

Then this Daniel distinguished himself above the governors and satraps, because an excellent spirit was in him; and the king gave thought to setting him over the whole realm.

It quickly became apparent that there was something special about Daniel. He had an excellent spirit, and everything that he did prospered. There were many who were jealous of him and wanted to bring him down. They could not get to him through his business transactions, so they determined that they could get to him through his relationship with his God.

Daniel 6:5 says:

Then these men said, "We shall not find any charge against this Daniel unless we find it against him concerning the law of his God."

They tricked the King into putting a decree together that for thirty days, no one could pray to any god but the image of the King, or they would be thrown into a den of hungry lions.

Daniel 6:6-9 goes on to say:

So these governors and satraps thronged before the king, and said thus to him: "King Darius, live forever! All the governors of the kingdom, the administrators and satraps, the counselors and advisors, have consulted together to establish a royal statute and to make a firm decree, that whoever petitions any god or man for thirty days, except you, O king, shall be cast into the den of lions. Now, O king, establish the decree and sign

---

the writing, so that it cannot be changed, according to the law of the Medes and Persians, which does not alter." Therefore King Darius signed the written decree.

They tricked King Darius into signing the decree. The King loved Daniel; Daniel was his right-hand man. And so, a law was created so that Daniel could not pray. However, Daniel went to his room and prayed three times a day anyway. He prayed in the morning, he prayed at noontime, he prayed in the evening. He was found guilty of violating this new law and was taken to the lion's den and left there overnight.

King Darius fasted and prayed for Daniel all night long. He tried to come up with a way to cancel his decree and save Daniel, but all his efforts fell short.

But we know how the story ends: Daniel rejoiced in his God and refused to worship anyone but the true God, and God delivered him.

God delivered Daniel, and he will deliver us. God put the lions to sleep, and Daniel was not harmed. God will quiet the sound of our trouble, too. If we will hold our peace, God will fight our battles and deliver us. If we will remain unmovable on the Word of God, God will deliver us as surely as He delivered Daniel.

The Weapon of Knowing

The battle is not our battle; the battle is the Lord's. But there are certain weapons God has given us. One of those weapons is the knowledge that we already have the victory. The weapon is knowing that the battle has already been won, that we have a sweatless victory.

This is the Kingdom of God. The Kingdom of God represents God's way of doing things.

Isaiah 55:8 says:

"For My thoughts are not your thoughts, Nor are your ways My ways," says the LORD.

Kingdom ways are not like our ways. We can only learn how to do things God's way by looking into the Word of God.

We are not ignorant of Satan's devices. God will show us the devil and all his evil ways.

Hosea 4:6 says:

My people are destroyed for lack of knowledge. Because you have rejected knowledge, I also will reject you from being priest for Me; Because you have forgotten the law of your God, I also will forget your children.

The Sound of Trouble

The Bible is not talking about the kind of knowledge that we might obtain from a university—it is talking about the kind of knowledge that comes from God. We can be destroyed by rejecting that knowledge when we receive it. The problem is not that knowledge is unavailable; the problem occurs when the knowledge God gives us is rejected.

Allow The Anointing To Teach You

The ways of God have to be taught. This is what going to church is all about: church is where we learn how to preserve our lives and live in the abundant life of God.

Psalm 27:11 says:

Teach me Your way, O LORD, And lead me in a smooth path, because of my enemies.

The Bible says that we have an anointing from God, and that it will teach us.

First John 2:20 says:

But you have an anointing from the Holy One, and you know all things.

We don't just get up one morning and know God's ways. We have to be taught God's ways under the anointing. God has anointed the fivefold ministry to do just that for us.

It is the anointing that lifts the heavy burdens and destroys the yoke.

Isaiah 10:27 says:

It shall come to pass in that day That his burden will be taken away from your shoulder, And his yoke from your neck, And the yoke will be destroyed because of the anointing oil.

When we allow the anointing to teach us, we will walk in victory, prosperity, health, and peace. The work of the enemy will be destroyed.

Psalm 27:12 says:

Do not deliver me to the will of my adversaries; For false witnesses have risen against me, And such as breathe out violence.

The false witnesses who testify, or speak words against us, are the ones who "*breathe out violence.*"

We need God to teach us how to deal with them. We need God to teach us how to deal with those who lie and threaten. We need God to show us what to say, and how to say it, to counteract the lies of the enemy.

The Sound of Trouble

Second Corinthians 10:4 says:

For the weapons of our warfare are not carnal, but mighty in God for pulling down strongholds.

He is going to teach us how to use these mighty weapons, but they can only be employed by using the Word of God.

The enemy is breathing out violence and we are breathing out anointing. John 7:38 says that, by the power of the Holy Spirit, out of our belly will flow *"rivers of living water."*

Through the Holy Spirit, we can speak life into dead situations. We can speak to the storms, and they will cease. We can speak to the mountains, and they will move out of our way. The mountain won't move and the storm won't be calmed when we only speak our own words: they have no power. The sound FOR trouble is the sound of God's Word.

Our Belief System

The sound FOR trouble is *to believe what we say*. Our belief in God's Word must be stronger than our belief in what we can see.

We have to believe in God's goodness. You have to find out what the Word of God says about His goodness.

Psalm 27:13 says:

I would have lost heart, unless I had believed That I would see the goodness of the LORD In the land of the living.

We have to know what we are looking for. Sometimes the goodness of God shows up and we don't even recognize it, because we don't know how to recognize His goodness. Goodness comes when Jesus shows up. In the time of trouble, Jesus will be right there—that's goodness! We need to learn how to recognize the goodness of the Lord.

Our belief system is based on God's Word. We will lose heart if we don't keep our belief system intact: we will fail; we will faint. We will not be strong enough to stand in the time of trouble.

The Word will strengthen us. All God asks us to do is to let the Word dwell in us richly—the Word will do the rest. All God asks is that we put His Word in our hearts.

We have to believe that we will see the goodness of the Lord in the land of the living. The enemy tries to ruin God's plan for our lives with the sounds of trouble he generates. But we have a solution for the sound of trouble: we can ask the Lord to teach us how to use His Word.

The Sound of Trouble

God's Word is powerful. When we speak God's Word, we are speaking with the power of God. Thus, God's Word is greater than whatever situation we may find ourselves in.

The centurion in Matthew 8:8 recognized the authority in Jesus' words. When he came to ask Jesus to heal his servant, he declared:

Lord, I am not worthy that You should come under my roof. But only speak a word, and my servant will be healed.

Jesus is the Word made manifest to us. We need to be like the centurion and respect the authority of the Word of God. If God's Word is spoken, there will be results. The Word works all the time because Jesus is the same today, yesterday, and forever.

The Antidote for the Sound of Trouble

When the bad report comes, we can follow in the centurion's footsteps. We can affirm that the spoken Word of God has the power to make a difference in our circumstances.

Here is what we can do: we can find the scriptures that pertain to our situation and begin to read them and rehearse them aloud.

There are many verses that apply to the troubles that are common to us all. Here are some scriptures to use as a starting point:

> For healing, use Isaiah 53:5: *But He was wounded for our transgressions, He was bruised for our iniquities; The chastisement for our peace was upon Him; And by his stripes we are healed.*

> For finances, use Deuteronomy 8:18: *"And you shall remember the LORD your God, for it is He who gives you power to get wealth, that He may establish His covenant which He swore to your fathers, as it is this day."*

> For peace, use Philippians 4:7: *And the peace of God, which surpasses all understanding, will guard your hearts and minds through Christ Jesus.*

The centurion understood that the Word was the antidote—the solution for his servant who was sick. He understood the power of the spoken Word.

When trouble strikes our homes, or when sickness hits our bodies, we can speak God's Word. He has already spoken it and released it to us. All we have to do is receive it and believe it.

The Sound of Trouble

Joshua 1:8 says:

This Book of the Law shall not depart from your mouth, but you shall meditate in it day and night, that you may observe to do according to all that is written in it. For then you will make your way prosperous, and then you will have good success.

We can't let up speaking the Word if we want to have good success. We have to take the words off the pages of the Bible and store them in our hearts. Then, we have to release them out of our mouths. We can practice meditating on that Word. We can practice saying what God says about our situation. We don't recite the sound of trouble; we respond with the sound of God's Word.

Though the sound of trouble comes at some point to us all, we are not without an antidote to the poisonous words and thoughts that our enemy uses against us. We have a powerful weapon ready to use at a moment's notice. We can speak God's Word and it will deflect the fiery darts of the enemy and bring us into victory!

We can turn the sound of trouble into the sound of triumph!

AFTERWORD

One of the most misunderstood principles of the Christian life is the fact that Christians can and will experience tests, trials, tribulations, and troubles until the Lord returns.

In this book, *The Sound of Trouble*, Bishop Tatuem establishes a proactive way of preparing for trouble, noting that before trouble arrives, there are indicators and warnings that we must not ignore, but to which we must properly respond.

This is a must-read. You have learned how you can walk in victory and never again be robbed of the inheritance that is rightfully yours in Christ! *Enjoy this book, and recommend it to others who will be blessed by it.*

Archbishop Ralph L. Dennis
Presiding Bishop
Kingdom Fellowship Covenant Ministries
Baltimore, Maryland

ABOUT THE AUTHOR

Bishop Roger L. Tatuem was born in Chase City, Virginia, but relocated to Maryland, where his ultimate destiny would be in ministry.

He was educated in the Harford County School System and is a graduate of Havre de Grace Consolidated School. He furthered his education by attending Essex, Dundalk, and Harford Community Colleges, where he completed training as a Chemical Abuse Counselor.

He was certified by the state of Maryland as an Alcoholism Counselor and was employed by Harford County Alcoholism Services as a Program Specialist. He was also awarded an Honorary Doctor of Divinity from Divine Bread of Life Bible College International, Baltimore, Maryland. Additionally, he is a Vietnam Veteran, having served in the United States Army.

Bishop Tatuem served faithfully at First Pentecostal Tabernacle Church in Elkton, Maryland, under the leadership of his Bishop (the late Bishop Huey L. Harris) and Mother Lou Ann Harris. It was during that time that he met the love of his life, Miriam L. Harris.

While serving at First Pentecostal Tabernacle Church, he accepted his call to the ministry and was united in marriage with Miriam. Their union has been blessed with one son, two daughters, eight grandchildren, and two great-grandchildren.

Bishop Tatuem was ordained as an Elder in the church, then released to become the founder of Helping Hands Ministries, in Churchville, Maryland. He was then consecrated as a Bishop. During this time, he was appointed as Regional Director of Maryland for World Harvest Church Ministerial Alliance Association under Dr. Rod Parsley (now known as City Harvest Network).

He is both an excellent teacher and preacher of the Word. Bishop Tatuem teaches a weekly Bible Study at Helping Hands Ministries in Churchville, conducts men's fellowship groups, and oversees the Helping Hands Ministries Bible Training Institute. His services can be seen on Streaming Live Weekly at www.hhministries.net, locally on Harford Cable Network, Harford County, and WMAR/ABC Channel 2, Baltimore, Maryland. His focus remains unchanged: "**Teaching Believers to Grow in the Word of God**."